WORSHIP TOGETHER.com®

Worship Resources For Your Generation

www.worshiptogether.com

Songbook 7.0

Songbook 7.0
Table of Contents

Title	Number

All Bow Down

Words and Music by
CHRIS TOMLIN and ED CASH

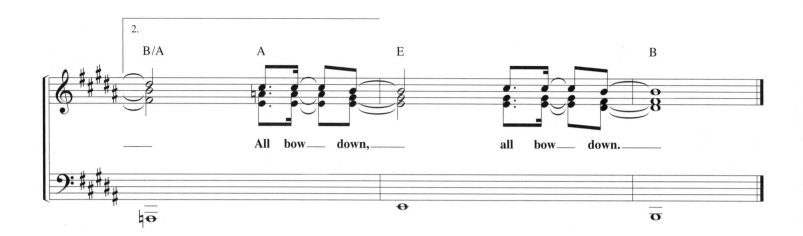

All bow— down,— all bow— down.—

Chords Used in This Song

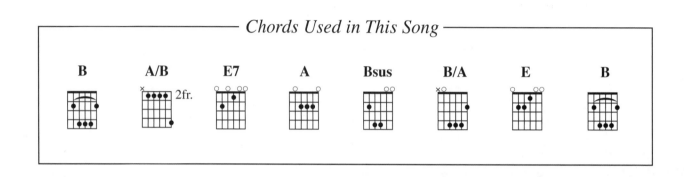

B   A/B   E7   A   Bsus   B/A   E   B

The Answer

Words and Music by
SHANE BARNARD

The Answer to the Question

Words and Music by
JOHN ELLIS

D.S. al CODA %

of earth and heav-en. How could they sing_____ a-bout ev-'ry -

thing_____ but_____ Him? He is the

all He says He is.

Chords Used in This Song

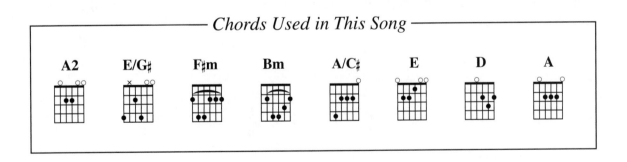

A2   E/G♯   F♯m   Bm   A/C♯   E   D   A

Beautiful One

Words and Music by
TIM HUGHES

CODA

My soul,_____ my soul_____ must sing._____ My soul,_____

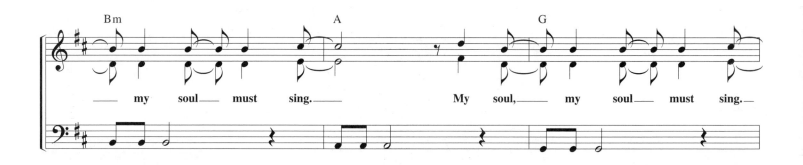

_____ my soul_____ must sing._____ My soul,_____ my soul_____ must sing._____

D.S. al Fine 𝄋

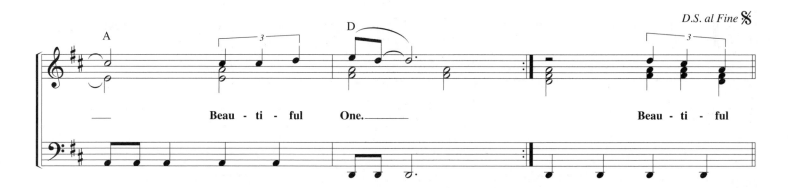

_____ Beau - ti - ful One._____ Beau - ti - ful

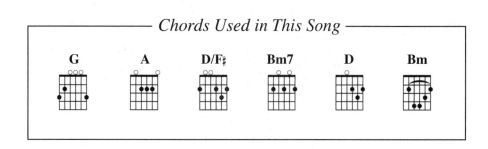

Chords Used in This Song

G   A   D/F♯   Bm7   D   Bm

Beauty for Ashes

6

Beauty of Your Peace

Words and Music by
TIM HUGHES

1. Your voice has stilled the rag - ing storms; The
(2. Bright) skies will soon be o - ve - rhead; We'll

wind and waves bow down be - fore. Your
en - ter in to Heav - en's rest. There'll

still small voice brings hope to all who
be no death, there'll be no pain, the

wait on You, we'll wait for You to
things of old will pass a - way. You'll

Chords Used in This Song

7

The Beauty of Simplicity

Words and Music by
JOSH WHITE

1.3. It's the beau-ty of sim-pli-ci-ty that brings me down to me knees.
2. It's the beau-ty of sim-pli-ci-ty that fills me with e-ter-ni-ty;

I'll praise You for e-ter-ni-ty. And Lord, I love You
I've tast-ed Your di-vin-i-ty. And Lord, I Love You

3rd time to CODA

Be-cause You, You first loved
Be-cause You, You first loved

1. me.
2. me. And all God's peo-ple say:

And all God's peo-ple say: We, _____ we love _____

B _____ F♯m _____ A

_____ You, _____ we love _____ You, Lord, _____ we love _____ You. _____ And we, _____

E _____ B _____ F♯m

_____ we love _____ You, _____ we love _____ You, Lord, _____ we love _____

1.
A

_____ You. _____ And

2.
A _____ E

_____ You, _____ we love _____ You.

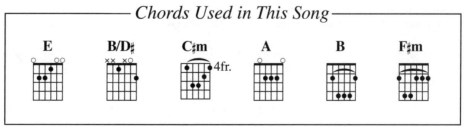

Breathing the Breath

Acts 17:25, Romans 11:35-36, James 1:17,
Psalm 50:9-12, 1 Chronicles 29:14

Words and Music by
MATT REDMAN

1. We have noth-ing to give that did-n't first come from Your hands. We have noth-ing to of-fer You which You did not pro-vide. Ev-'ry good per-fect gift comes from Your kind and gra-cious heart, and all

2. Who has giv-en to You that it should be paid back to Him? Who has giv-en to You as if You need-ed an-y-thing? From You, and to You, and through You come all things O Lord, and all

CODA

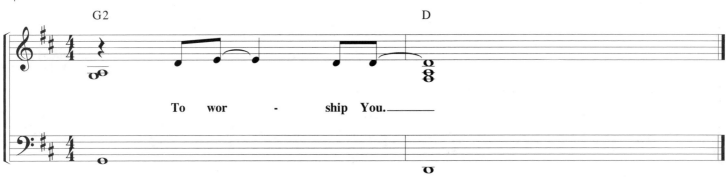

To wor - ship You._____

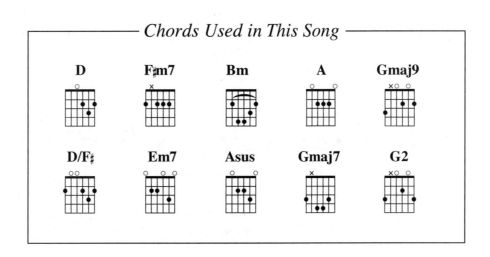

9

Consuming Fire

Words and Music by
TIM HUGHES

1. There must be more___ than this:___ O breath of God___ come breathe___ with-in.___ There must be more___ than this:___ Spir-it of God___ we wait___ for You.___ Fill us a-new,___ we pray;___ fill us a-new, we pray.

2. Come like a rush-ing wind,___ clothe us in pow-er from___ on high.___ Now set the cap-tives free;___ Leave us a-ban-doned to___ Your praise.___ Lord, let Your glo-ry fall.___ Lord, let Your glo-ry fall.

Con - sum - ing Fire, fan in - to flame a

pas - sion for Your name. Spi - rit of God, fall in this

place. Lord, have Your way, Lord, have Your way with us.

Chords Used in This Song

F#m7 E/G# A D A/C# E Bm7

Bless the Lord

Words and Music by
JEFF DEYO

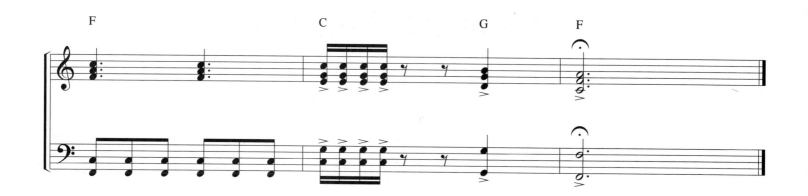

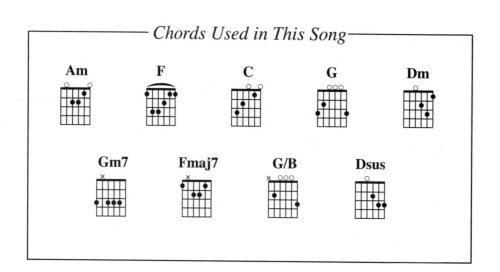

Chords Used in This Song

11

Created to Worship

Words and Music by
VICKY BEECHING

1. You formed us from the dust, You breathed Your breath
2. If we don't wor-ship You, we'll search for sub-

— in us. We are the work of Your hands.
-sti-tutes to fill the void in our souls.

— to You love songs of grat-i-tude,
-er things de-stroys our lib-er-ty.

Now we breathe back
Wor-ship-ing oth-

C♯m7

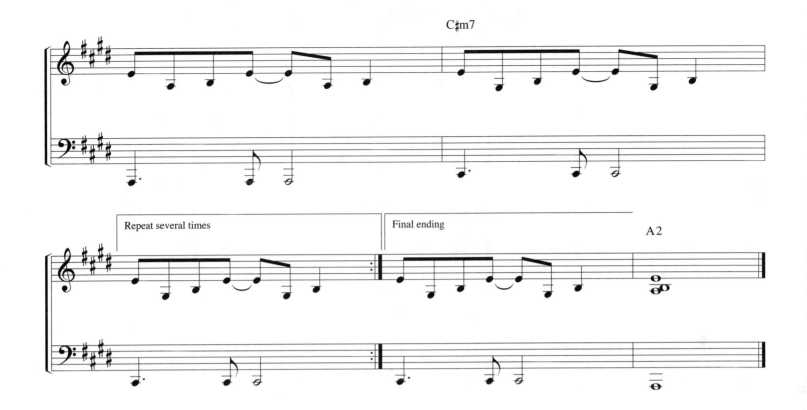

Repeat several times

Final ending

A2

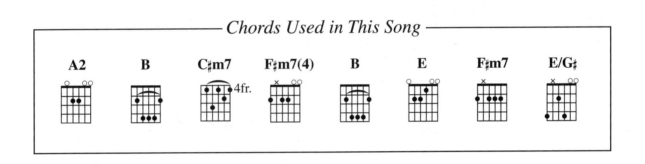

Chords Used in This Song

| A2 | B | C♯m7 | F♯m7(4) | B | E | F♯m7 | E/G♯ |

12

Cry in My Heart

Words and Music by
TIM NEUFELD
and JON NEUFELD

2nd time to CODA ⊕

2.

D   A

\- ry,_____ You are the lift - er of____ my

Bm   G

head,_____ lift - er of___ this____

Bm   G   A   D

___ head.____   Yeah.

Chords Used in This Song

D   A   Em7   Asus   G   D/F♯   Bm

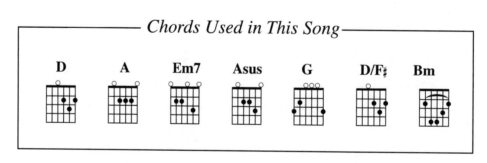

13

Every Little Thing

Words and Music by
STUART GARRARD
and MARTIN SMITH

14

Dancing Generation

Words and Music by
MATT REDMAN

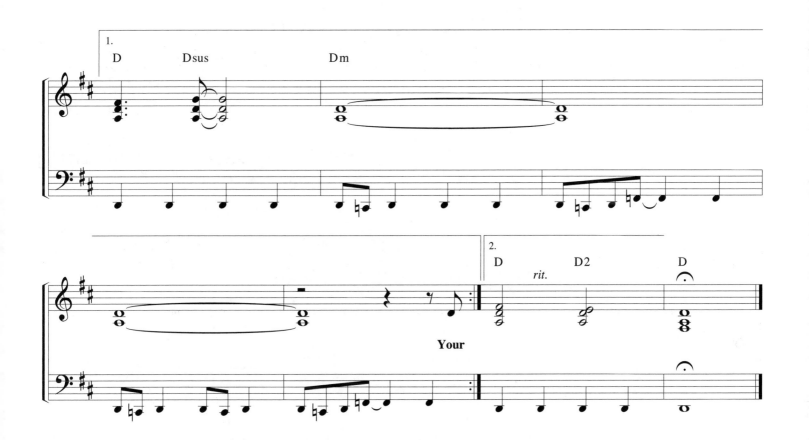

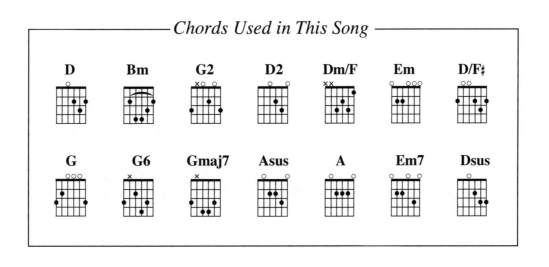

Chords Used in This Song

15

Divine Invitation

Words and Music by
ERIC OWYOUNG and
STEVE HINDALONG

1. Sweet, sweet love of God. We re-vere Your fi-re-light heart.
2. Sweet, sweet Sav-ior come near us now in-to the depths of our hearts.

Sweet, sweet grace sur-rounds; We've been sought
Sweet, sweet breath of life, You ful-fill

through all of our years. You've car-ried our tears with You.
with the warmth of Your love, the mys-ter-y of Your ways.

We are all here to find the place where our rest-

for our souls——— where the long - ings were born——— long a - go,———

for our souls——— where the long - ings were born——— long a - go.———

Chords Used in This Song

| D | G | Bm | A | D/A | Bm7 | D/G | G2 |

16

Empty Me

Words and Music by
**JOHN MARK COMER
and GENE WAY**

17

Everyone Knows

Words and Music by
STUART GARRARD
and MARTIN SMITH

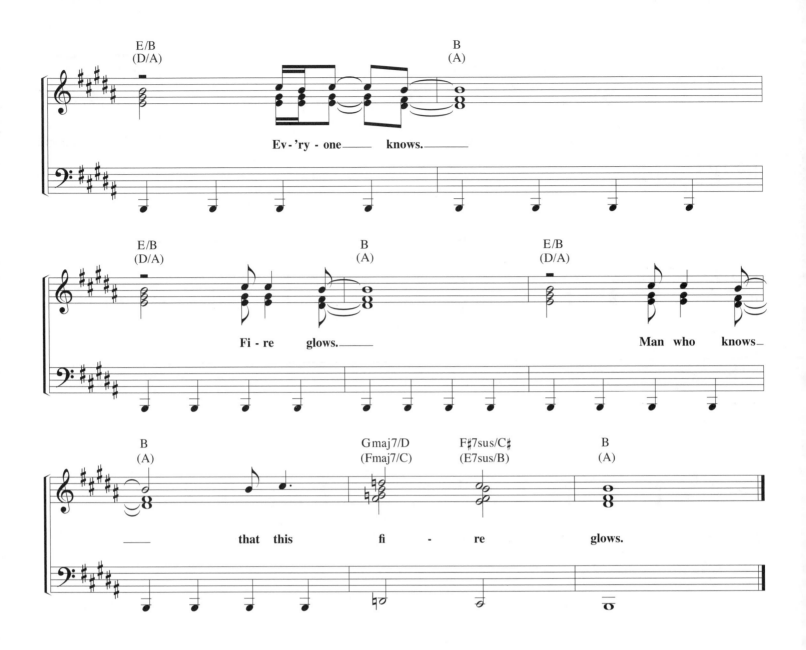

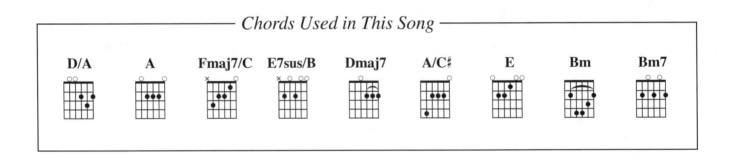

Chords Used in This Song

Facedown

Leviticus 9:24

**Words and Music by
MATT and BETH REDMAN**

Chords Used in This Song

Feel It Comin' On

Words and Music by
STUART GARRARD
and MARTIN SMITH

D.S. al CODA %

Φ CODA

me to - night?

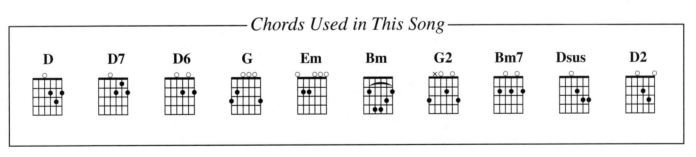

20

Forever

Words and Music by
**SARAH KELLY, DANIEL HUSCROFT
and MICHAEL PAYNE**

noth - ing can change Your love; ____ it's mine for -

ev - er. _____ And

noth - ing can steal my heart; ____ it's Yours for -

2nd and 3rd times to CODA ⊕

ev - er. _____

2. Touched by Your hand ____ of grace, ____

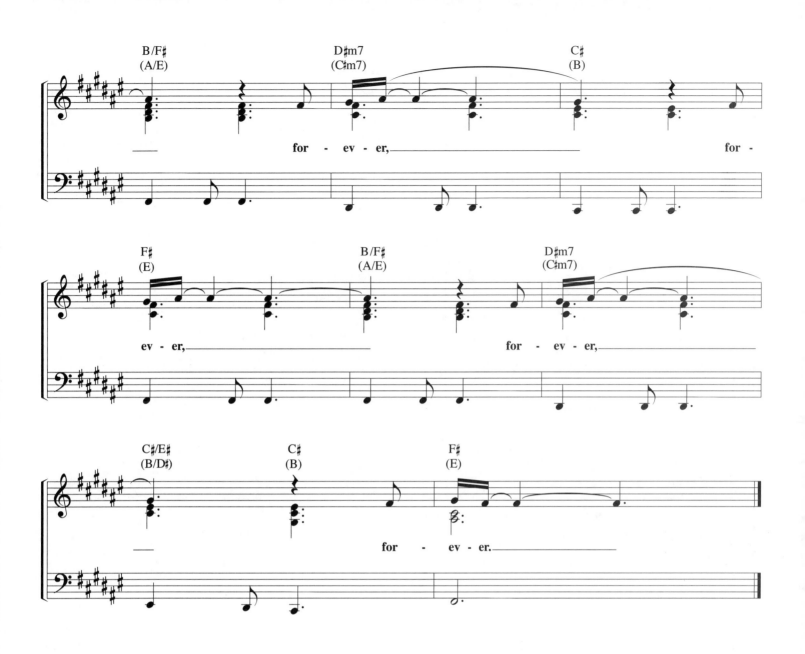

for - ev - er,_____ for -

ev - er,_____ for - ev - er,_____

for - ev - er._____

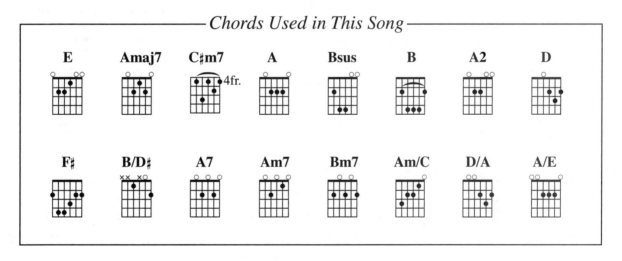

Chords Used in This Song

E Amaj7 C#m7 A Bsus B A2 D

F# B/D# A7 Am7 Bm7 Am/C D/A A/E

21

Free

Words and Music by
STUART GARRAD, MARTIN SMITH
and JOHN THATCHER

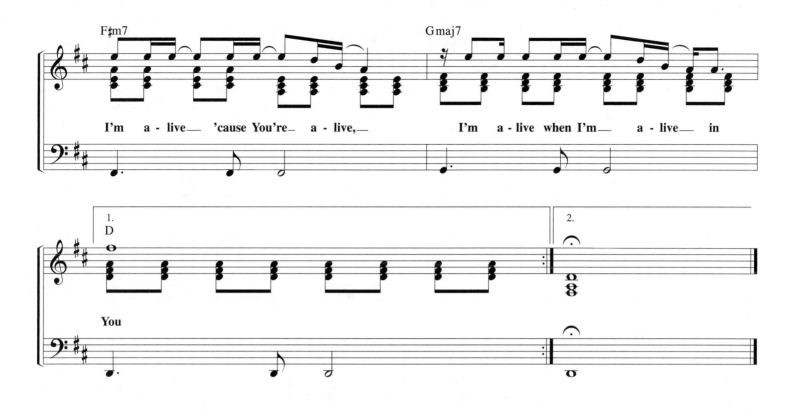

I'm a - live— 'cause You're— a - live,— I'm a - live when I'm— a - live— in

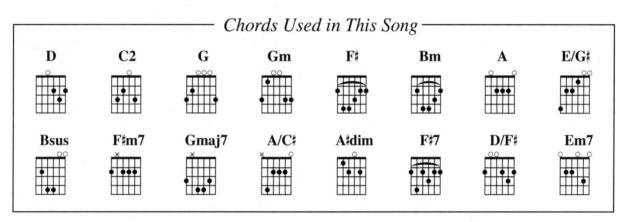

1.
D

You

2.

```
┌──────────── Chords Used in This Song ────────────┐
│                                                    │
│   D      C2     G      Gm     F#     Bm    A    E/G#│
│                                                    │
│  Bsus   F#m7  Gmaj7   A/C#   A#dim   F#7   D/F#  Em7│
│                                                    │
└────────────────────────────────────────────────────┘
```

Filled with Your Glory

Words and Music by
TIM and JON NEUFELD

Gifted Response
(We Will Worship You)

Hebrews 12:22, Psalm 66:2

Words and Music by
MATT REDMAN

Chords Used in This Song

D2 D2aug Em7 D/F♯ G2 Asus Gm6 D

Giver of Life

Words and Music by
TIM HUGHES

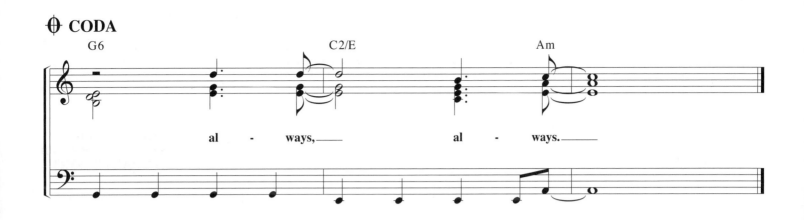

al - ways,_____ al - ways._____

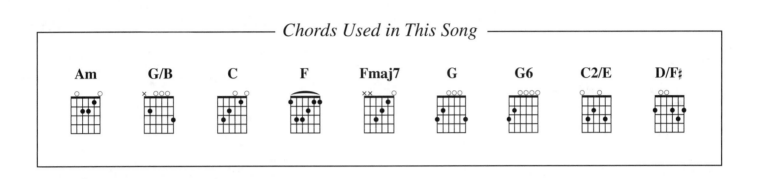

Chords Used in This Song

Am   G/B   C   F   Fmaj7   G   G6   C2/E   D/F♯

God In Heaven

Words and Music by
STUART GARRARD
and MARTIN SMITH

__ my Sav - iour, He__ has done__ and great - er things are yet__

__ to come.__ Great things ____ to come.__

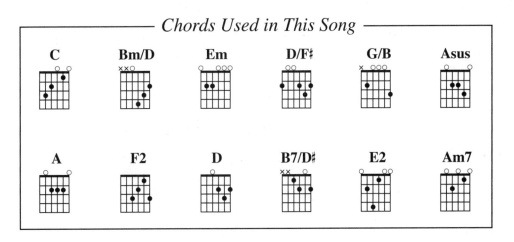

Chords Used in This Song

C   Bm/D   Em   D/F#   G/B   Asus

A   F2   D   B7/D#   E2   Am7

26

Grace Like a River

Words and Music by
STUART GARRARD
and MARTIN SMITH

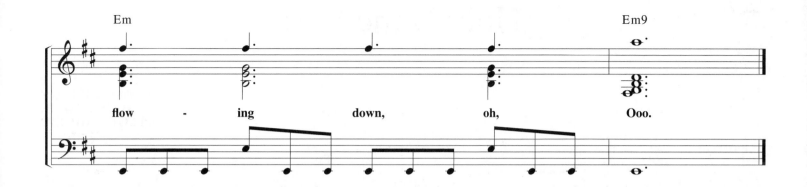

flow - ing down, oh, Ooo.

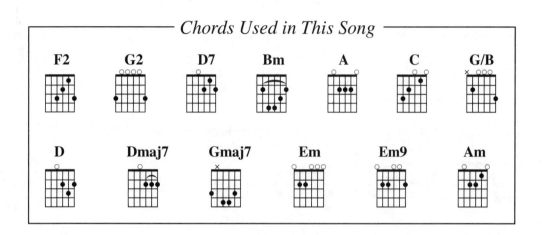

Chords Used in This Song

F2   G2   D7   Bm   A   C   G/B

D   Dmaj7   Gmaj7   Em   Em9   Am

Holy Is the Lord

Words and Music by
CHRIS TOMLIN
and LOUIE GIGLIO

Chords Used in This Song

Holy, Holy

Words and Music by
NATHAN FELLINGHAM

2nd time to CODA

How Great Is Our God

Words and Music by
**CHRIS TOMLIN, JESSE REEVES
and ED CASH**

is our God!

How great

⊕ CODA

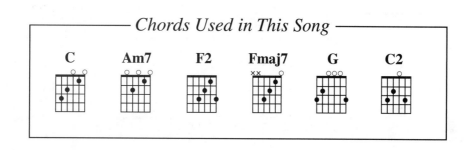

is our God!

Chords Used in This Song

C Am7 F2 Fmaj7 G C2

30

I Stand For You

Words and Music by
JOHN ELLIS

Glory

**Words and Music by
HECTOR CERBANTES
and MARK HALL**

Capo 2 (E)   ♩ = 120

Keyboard
(Guitar)

You are ho-ly in this place. You are wor-thy of my praise, and we wor-ship You. Je-sus, we wor-ship You. You're the King of kings and the Lord of lords. You're the Mas-ter of

I Surrender to You

Words and Music by
**ANDY DODD, ADAM WATTS
and GANNIN ARNOLD**

1. — Lord, You live in me, — You're my best friend. — You're the King of Kings, — the be-gin-ning and end. — — Now that You have my eyes, I see Your Spir-it in-side — — of me.

2. You hold the key to my life — in Your lov-ing hands. Al-ways by my side, I of-fer all that I am. So glad I re-al-ize You are the truth and the light — in my life.

CODA

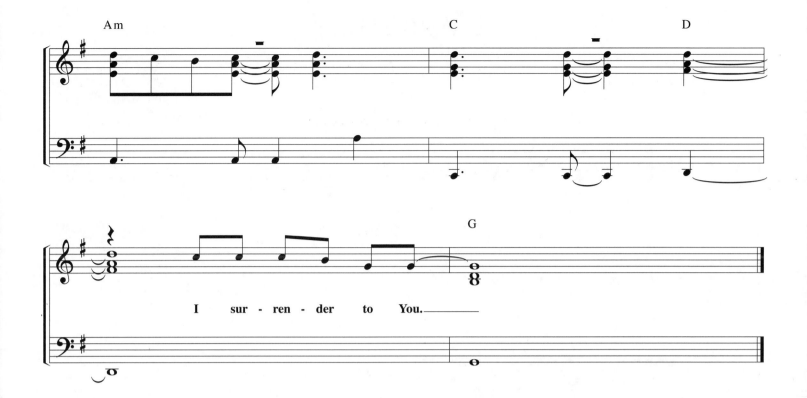

I sur - ren - der to You._____

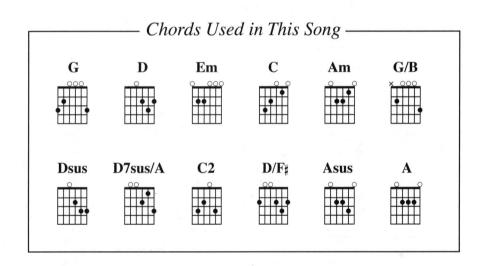

Chords Used in This Song

| G | D | Em | C | Am | G/B |

| Dsus | D7sus/A | C2 | D/F♯ | Asus | A |

I Was Blind

Words and Music by
STUART GARRARD
and MARTIN SMITH

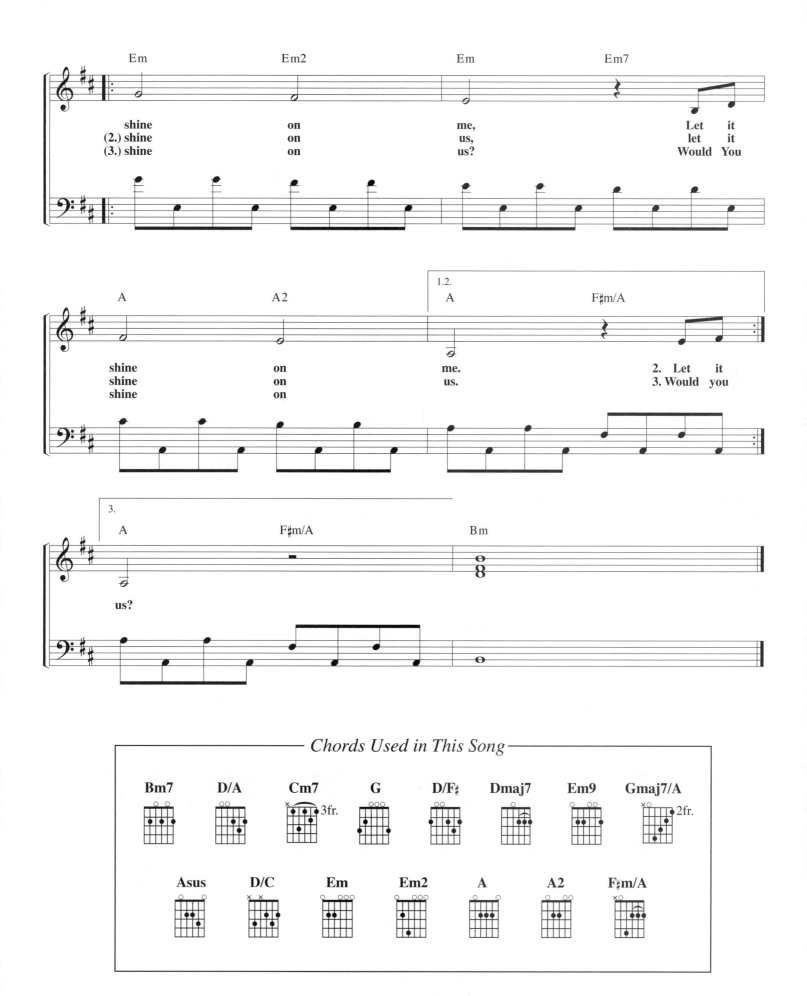

If I Have Not Love

1 Corithians 13:1-3

Words and Music by
MATT REDMAN

Chords Used in This Song

If We Are the Body

Music by
MARK HALL

Music by
CASTING CROWNS

2nd time to CODA ⊕
3rd time to CODA ⊕ ⊕

why aren't His feet___ go - ing? Why is___ His love

___ not show - ing them___ there is___ a way?___

There is___ a way.___

2. A trav - 'ler___ is

far a - way___ from home.___

He sheds___ his coat___

E

for us to pick and choose who should come___ And we are the bod-

F♯m   D2   *D.S. al CODA* 𝄋

-y___ of Christ___   If

CODA

D2   F♯m

Je - sus is___ the way.___

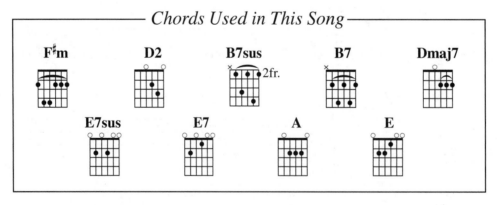

Chords Used in This Song

F♯m   D2   B7sus   B7   Dmaj7

E7sus   E7   A   E

Indescribable

Words and Music by
LAURA STORY
Additional lyrics by **JESSE REEVES**

Chords Used in This Song

Inside Outside

Joy Is in This Place

Words and Music by
TIM HUGHES

King

Capo 1 (D)

♩ = 144

Words and Music by
JOHN ELLIS

King of Glory

Words and Music by
CHRIS TOMLIN and JESSE REEVES

Chords Used in This Song

G   C2   Em7   D

Lead Us Up the Mountain

Words and Music by
MATT REDMAN

Capo 2 (E) ♩ = 76

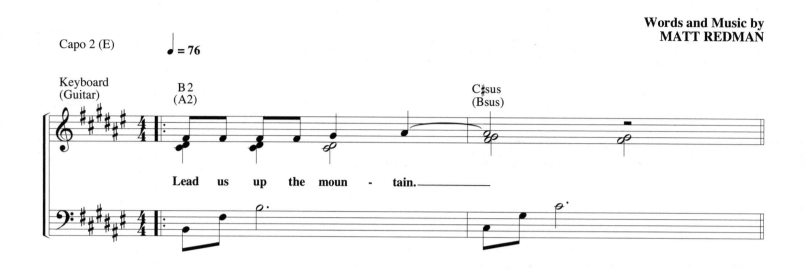

Lead us up the moun - tain.

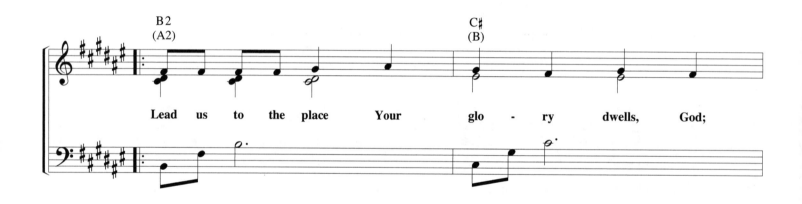

Lead us to the place Your glo - ry dwells, God;

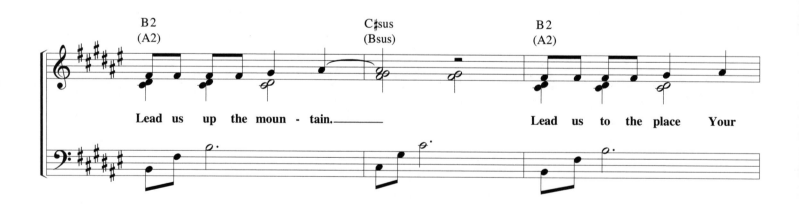

Lead us up the moun - tain. Lead us to the place Your

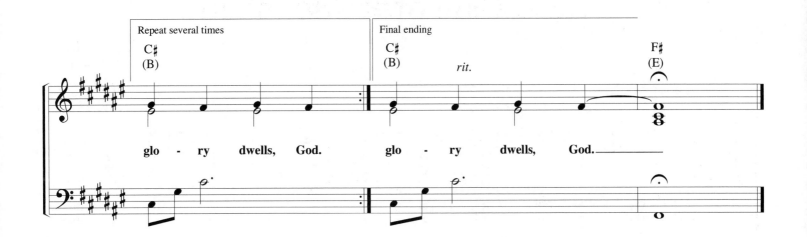

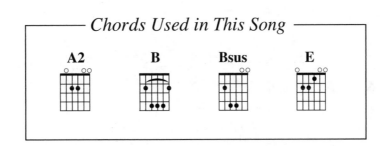

Life of Praise

Words and Music by
MARK HALL

2. I will ___ You're wor -

- thy of ___ my praise.

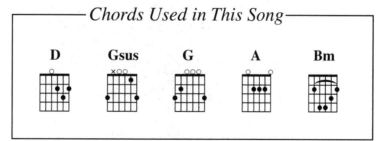

Majesty

Words and Music by
MARTIN SMITH and
STUART GARRARD

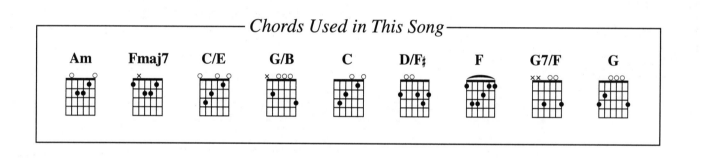

Chords Used in This Song

Living Hallelujah

Words and Music by
SARAH KELLY

Mighty Is the Power of the Cross

Words and Music by
CHRIS TOMLIN, SEAN CRAIG
and JESSE REEVES

Mission's Flame

Revelation 5:9

Words and Music by
MATT REDMAN

send us out._____

Send___ us

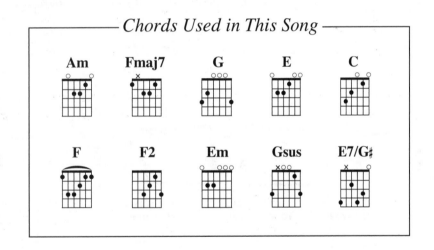

Chords Used in This Song

Am Fmaj7 G E C

F F2 Em Gsus E7/G#

Mountains High

Words and Music by
MARTIN SMITH

48

Name Above All Names

Words and Music by
TIM HUGHES

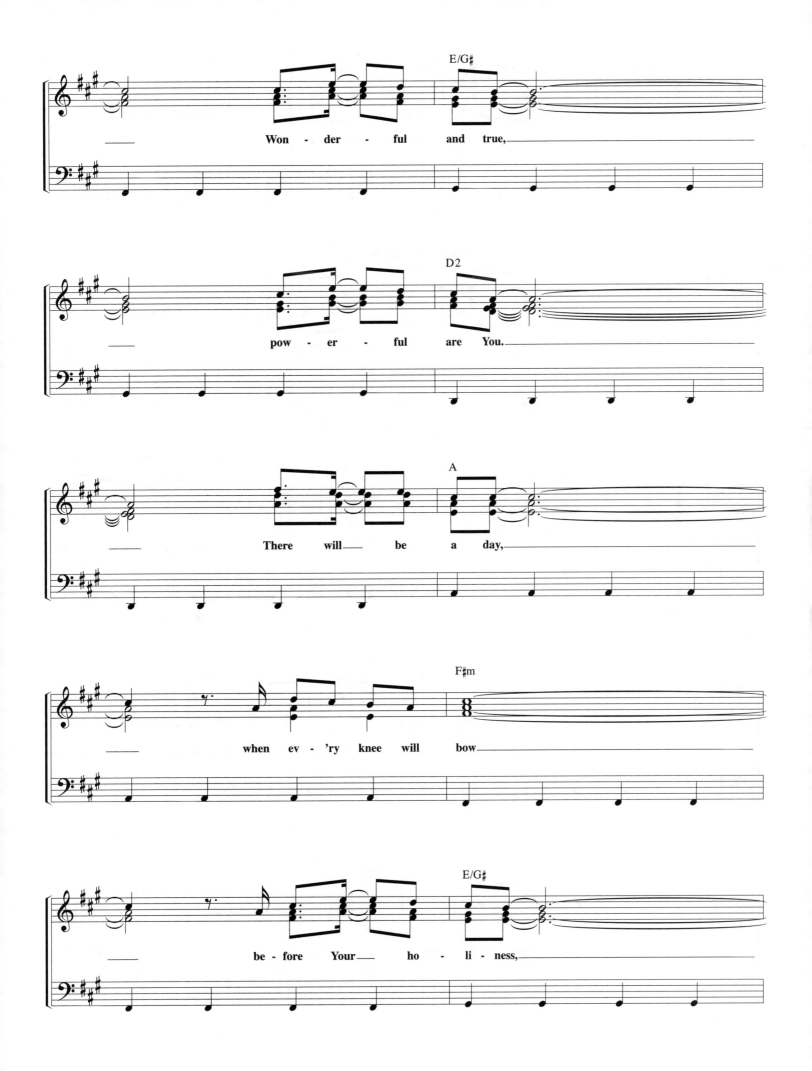

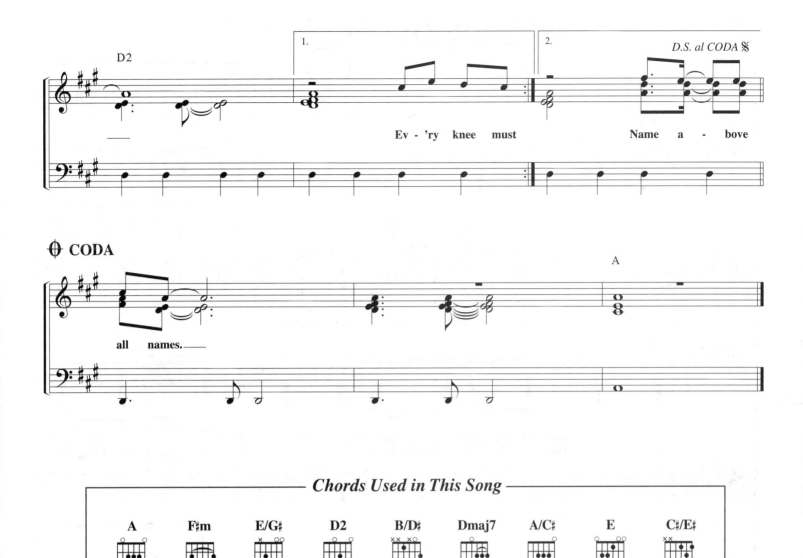

Chords Used in This Song

A F#m E/G# D2 B/D# Dmaj7 A/C# E C#/E#

Nothing But the Blood

Capo 2 (A) ♩ = 80

Words and Music by
MATT REDMAN

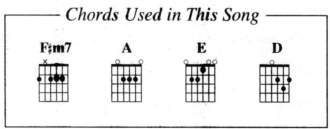

On Our Side

Words and Music by
ED CASH, JESSE REEVES
and CHRIS TOMLIN

⊕ CODA

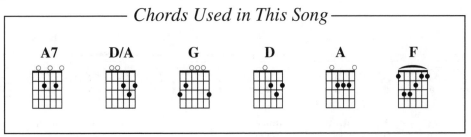

noth-in' gon-na stand in our way.

Chords Used in This Song

A7 D/A G D A F

51

Nothing in This World

Words and Music by
TIM HUGHES

1. Noth - ing in this world, no
(2.) place with - in my heart a

treas - ure man could buy, could take the place of
fire that burns for You, that wa - ters can - not

draw - ing near to—— You. There's
quench nor wash a - way. And

noth - ing I want more than to spend my days with
let that fi - re blaze —— through all e - ter - ni -

Chords Used in This Song

52

Praise Awaits You

Psalm 65:1

Words and Music by
MATT REDMAN

wake, and we'll sing 'til the break of the day, be-cause You

are wor-thy, yes, Lord!

3rd time to CODA ⊕

We're

read-y to re-spond to the glo-ries of Your name,

to the won-ders—— of Your heart,

Your great love.————

We're Your great love.————

D.S. al CODA 𝄋

CODA

Chords Used in This Song

53 Presence
(My Heart's Desire)

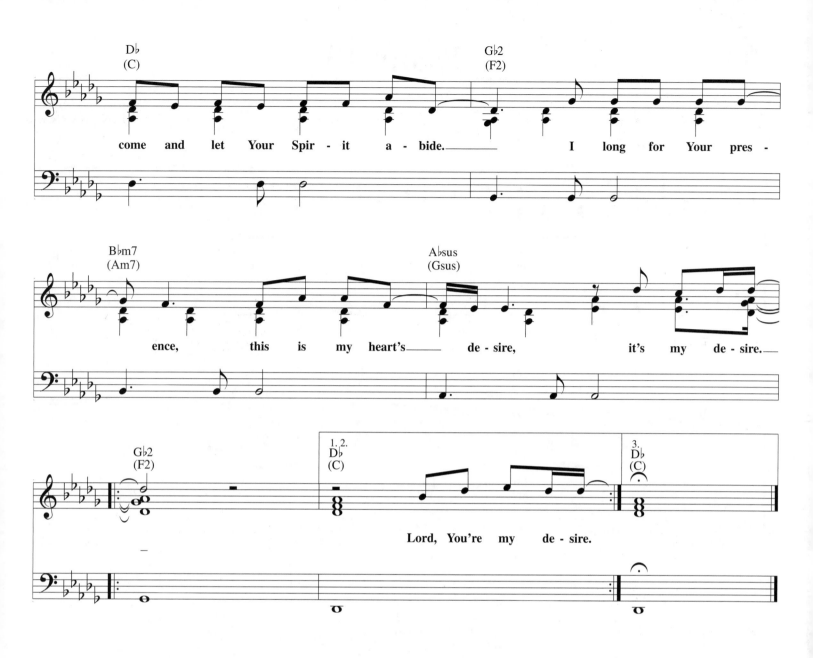

come and let Your Spir - it a - bide._____ I long for Your pres -

ence, this is my heart's_____ de - sire, it's my de - sire._____

Lord, You're my de - sire.

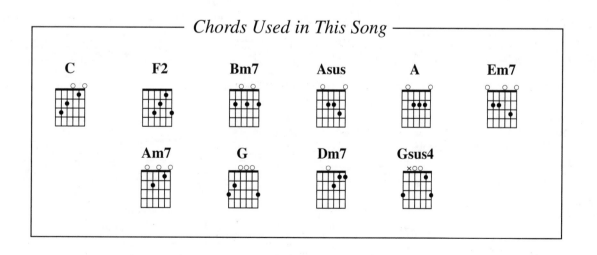

Chords Used in This Song

Psalm 13

Capo 1 (Am)

Words and Music by
SHANE BARNARD

Pure Light

Revelation 1:17

Words and Music by
LOUIE GIGLIO
and MATT REDMAN

1. ___ O to see ___ You as ___ You are, ___ to glimpse the won -
(2. How great the glo) - ry of ___ Your name, ___ how small the voice

- ders yet ___ un - seen. ___ As - sist my sight, ___ un - veil my eyes ___ ___ to see
___ I hum - bly bring. ___ Yet, with my all ___ I raise a song ___ when I see

___ You. ___ ___ Lord, to know ___ You as ___ You are, ___ to e - ven dare -
___ You. It is the song ___ of love's pure light, ___ the grace ___ re - flect -

___ to speak ___ or stand; Though marked be - loved, ___ to fall as dead ___ when I see
- ed in ___ these eyes, ___ the o - ver - flow ___ of those who know ___ they have seen

Lord,— in Your— pure light.—

Chords Used in This Song

56

Rain Down

Words and Music by
MARTIN SMITH and STUART GARRARD

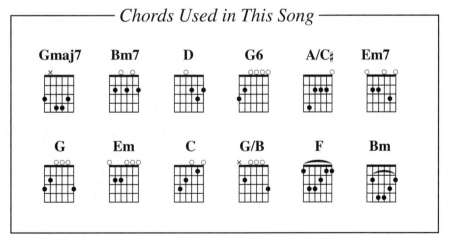

Seeing You

Words and Music by
MATT REDMAN

*NOTE: For authentic "drop D" chord voicing version visit www.mattredman.com

Spirit Waltz

Words and Music by
ERIC OWYOUNG

Strong Tower

Words and Music by
**PETER FURLER and
STEVE TAYLOR**

♩ = 80

1. Strong and might - y,____ strong to save us,____ like a
for - tress____ nev - er fail - ing.____ Strong in bat - tle,____ strong in
lead us____ through the

kind - ness,____ when we stray, Lord,____ You're strong to find us.____ When the
sha - dows,____ strong to car - ry____ all our sor - rows.____ When the

winds come hard a - gainst____ us____ You are stead - fast You are true.____ When the
en - e - my sur - rounds____ us,____ clos - ing in as dark - ness falls.____ Though his

60

Unfailing Love

Words and Music by
CHRIS TOMLIN, CARY PIERCE
and ED CASH

Praise You, God of earth and sky, how beau-ti-ful is Your un-fail-ing love, un-fail-ing love. And You nev-er change, God, You re-main the Ho-ly One and my un-fail-ing love, un-fail-ing love. You are my love.

Chords Used in This Song

G   C   G/B   Am7   D   Dsus   G/F#   Em7

61

Walk By Faith

Copyright © 2002 Thirsty Moon River Publishing, Inc./Stolen Pride (adm. by EMI Christian Music Publishing).

⊕ CODA

Chords Used in This Song

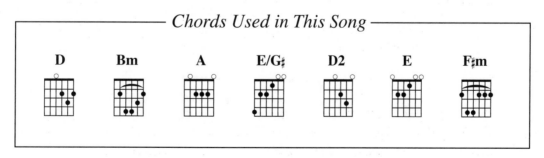

62

The Way I Was Made

Words and Music by
ED CASH, JESSE REEVES
and CHRIS TOMLIN

1. Caught in the half - light,____ I'm caught____ a - lone;____ ____ to the sun - rise,____ Feels like I'm tied____ up,

2. Made in Your like - ness,____ ____ made with Your hands,____ - cov - er who____ You are____ All I've for - got - ten,

Wak - ing up____ made to dis - and the ra - di - o.____ ten,

63

When I Search

Words and Music by
ERIC OWYOUNG

with - in Your love.

When I search for You,

ev - e - ry day I find how whole You make me. When I

lay down___ all of my will,___ I am found___

with - in___ When I search___ with - in___ Your___ love.___

Chords Used in This Song

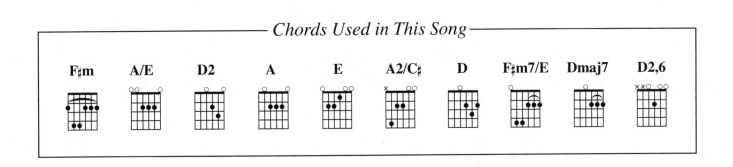

F♯m   A/E   D2   A   E   A2/C♯   D   F♯m7/E   Dmaj7   D2,6

When the Tears Fall

Words and Music by
TIM HUGHES

Who Am I

Words and Music by
MARK HALL and
CASTING CROWNS

2. Who am I,——

I   am   Yours.——

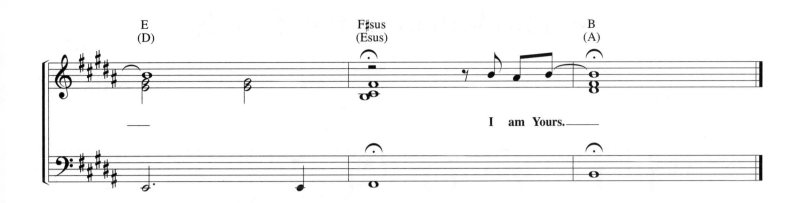

I am Yours.

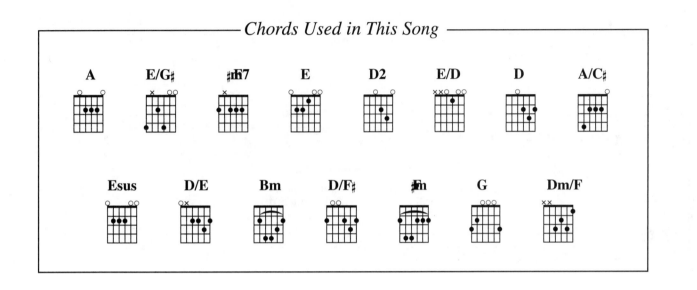

Chords Used in This Song

66

Whole World in His Hands

Words and Music by
TIM HUGHES

1. When all a-round is fad - ing,
2. When I walk through fi - re,

and noth - ing seems to last,
I will not be burned;

when each day is filled with sor - row, still I
When the waves come crash - ing 'round me, still I

know with all my heart:
know with all my heart:

With You

Words and Music by
STUART GARRARD
and MARTIN SMITH

Chords Used in This Song

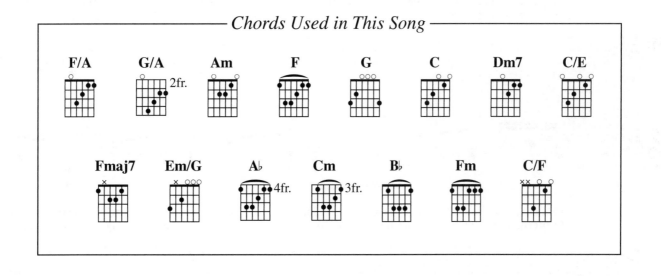

F/A   G/A   Am   F   G   C   Dm7   C/E

Fmaj7   Em/G   A♭   Cm   B♭   Fm   C/F

68 Worthy, You Are Worthy

Revelation 4:11, Job 42:5

Words and Music by
MATT REDMAN

1. Wor-thy, You are wor-thy,___ much more wor-thy than I know.___
2. Glo-ry, I give glo-ry___ to the One who saved my soul.___ You

I can-not i-mag-ine___ just how glo-ri-ous___ You are,
found me and you freed me___ from the shame that was___ my own.

and I can-not be-gin___ to tell___ how deep a love___ You bring.
And I can-not be-gin___ to tell___ how mer-ci-ful___ You've been.

O Lord, my ears had heard of You,___ but now my eyes have
O Lord, my ears had heard of You,___ but now my eyes have

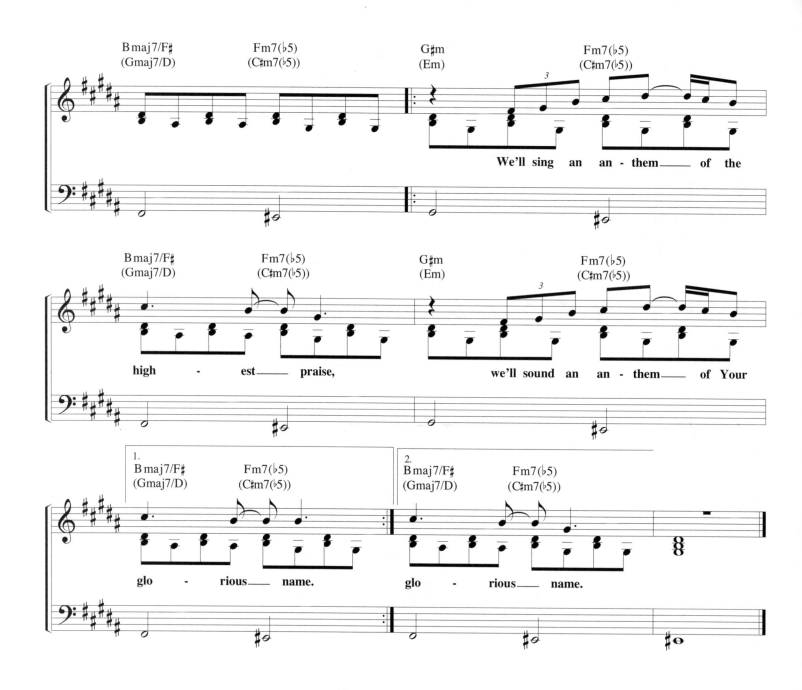

We'll sing an an-them_____ of the

high - est_____ praise, we'll sound an an - them_____ of Your

1.
glo - rious_____ name.

2.
glo - rious_____ name.

Chords Used in This Song

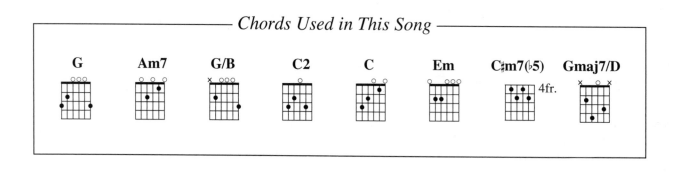

G Am7 G/B C2 C Em C#m7(♭5) Gmaj7/D

Yahweh

Words and Music by
SHAWN McDONALD

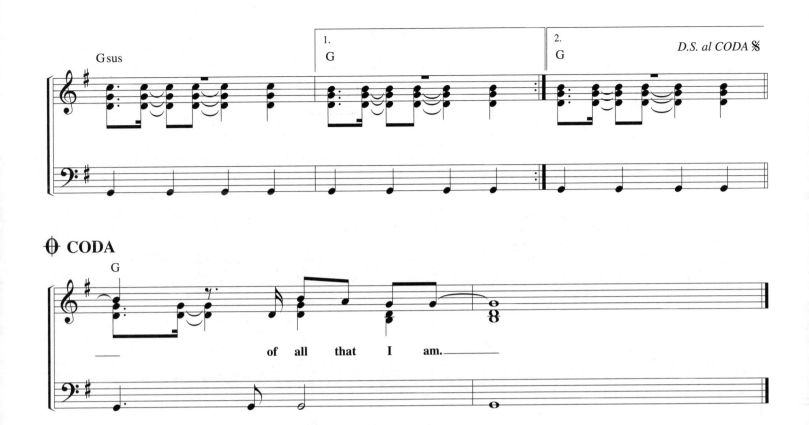

D.S. al CODA %

⊕ CODA

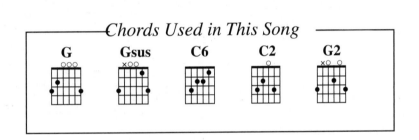

of all that I am.____

Chords Used in This Song

| G | Gsus | C6 | C2 | G2 |

You

Words and Music by
TIM HUGHES, ROB HILL
and JON MANN-SMITH

You Do All Things Well

Words and Music by
**CHRIS TOMLIN, MICHAEL JOHN CLEMENT
and JESSE REEVES**

1. Moun - tain mak - er, o - cean tam - er,
2. Star cre - at - or, wind breath -

- er, glimps - es of You burn in my eyes.
- er, the strokes of Your beau - ty brushed through the clouds,

The wor - ship of heav - en fills up the skies. You made it all;
light from the heav - ens touch - ing the ground.

Said, "Let there be," and there was all that we see.

Chords Used in This Song

72

Your Grace Is Enough

Words and Music by
MATT MAHER
Additional lyrics by
CHRIS TOMLIN

1. Great is___ Your faith - ful - ness,___ oh God.___
2. Great is___ your love___ and jus - tice, God.___

You wres - tle with___ the sin - ner's heart,___
You use___ the weak___ to lead___ the strong,___

You lead___ us by___
You lead___ us in___

___ still wa - ters in - to mer - cy,
___ the song___ of Your___ sal - va - tion,

I'm cov - ered in _____ Your love. _____

Your grace is e - nough _____ for _____ me, _____

for _____ me. _____

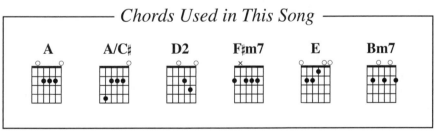

Chords Used in This Song

A   A/C♯   D2   F♯m7   E   Bm7

Index of Songs by Key

Title	Number	Capo	Played Key

Key of A♭

Title	Number	Capo	Played Key
Filled With Your Glory	22	1	G
Unfailing Love	60	1	G

Key of A

Title	Number	Capo	Played Key
Consuming Fire	9		
Name Above All Names	48		
When I Search	63		
Your Grace Is Enough	72		

Key of Am

Title	Number	Capo	Played Key
Giver Of Life	24		

Key of B♭

Title	Number	Capo	Played Key
Holy Is The Lord	27	1	A
On Our Side	50	1	A
Walk By Faith	61	1	A

Key of B♭m

Title	Number	Capo	Played Key
Psalm 13	54	1	Am

Key of B

Title	Number	Capo	Played Key
All Bow Down	1		
The Answer to the Question	3	2	A
Everyone Knows	17	2	A
Indescribable	36	2	A
Nothing But The Blood	49	2	A
Praise Awaits You	52	2	A
Who Am I	65	2	A
Worthy, You Are Worthy	68	4	G

Key of Bm

Title	Number	Capo	Played Key
Mission's Flame	46	2	Am

Key of C

Title	Number	Capo	Played Key
Beauty Of Your Peace	6		
Bless the Lord	10		
Mountains High	47		
Spirit Waltz	58		
The Way I Was Made	62		
With You	67		

Title	Number	Capo	Played Key

Key of D♭

How Great Is Our God	29	1	C
Inside Outside	37	1	C
Majesty (Here I Am)	43	1	C
Presence	53	1	C

Key of D

Beautiful One	4
Breathing The Breath	8
Cry In My Heart	12
Dancing Generation	14
Divine Invitation	15
Feel It Coming On	19
Free	21
Gifted Response (We Will Worship You)	23
Grace Like A River	26
I Stand For You	30
I Was Blind	33
Joy In This Place	38
Life Of Praise	42
Pure Light	55
Rain Down	56
Seeing You	57
When the Tears Fall	64
Whole World In His Hands	66
You Do All Things Well	71

Key of E♭

Beauty for Ashes	5	1	D
King	39	1	D

Key of E

The Answer	2
The Beauty of Simplicity	7
Created to Worship	11
If I Have Not Love	34
Living Hallelujah	44
Nothing In This World	51

Key of F♯

Empty Me	16	2	E
Forever	20	2	E
Glory	31	2	E
Lead Us Up The Mountain	41	2	E

Title	Number	Capo	Played Key

Index of Songs by Tempo

Title	Number	MM	Time Signature
Up-tempo			
King	39	144	4/4
Feel It Coming On	19	140	4/4
Dancing Generation	14	138	4/4
With You	67	132	4/4
Rain Down	56	128	4/4
Breathing The Breath	8	126	4/4
If We Are The Body	35	126	4/4
Joy In This Place	38	126	4/4
Beautiful One	4	120	4/4
Filled With Your Glory	22	120	4/4
Giver Of Life	24	120	4/4
Glory	31	120	4/4
Name Above All Names	48	120	4/4
When I Search	63	120	4/4
You	70	120	4/4
Your Grace Is Enough	72	120	4/4
Created to Worship	11	116	4/4
God In Heaven	25	116	4/4
Seeing You	57	116	4/4
Indescribable	36	dotted quarter = 60	6/8
Mid up-tempo			
The Answer	2	112	4/4
Inside Outside	37	112	4/4
Life Of Praise	42	112	4/4
Praise Awaits You	52	112	4/4
The Way I Was Made	62	112	4/4
Mission's Flame	46	102	4/4
All Bow Down	1	100	4/4
King Of Glory	40	100	4/4
Everyone Knows	17	98	4/4
Bless the Lord	10	dotted quarter = 54	6/8
Forever	20	dotted quarter = 52	6/8
Walk By Faith	61	dotted quarter = 51	6/8
Gifted Response (We Will Worship You)	23	dotted quarter = 50	6/8
Mid-tempo			
Free	21	92	4/4
Holy, Holy	28	88	4/4
I Stand For You	30	88	4/4
On Our Side	50	88	4/4
Psalm 13	54	86	4/4
Holy Is The Lord	27	84	4/4
You Do All Things Well	71	84	4/4

Title	Number	MM	Time Signature
The Answer to the Question	3	80	4/4
Nothing But The Blood	49	80	4/4
Nothing In This World	51	80	4/4
Presence	53	80	4/4
Strong Tower	59	80	4/4

Slow mid-tempo

Title	Number	MM	Time Signature
Consuming Fire	9	76	4/4
Cry In My Heart	12	76	4/4
Empty Me	16	76	4/4
Facedown	18	76	4/4
Grace Like A River	26	76	12/8
How Great Is Our God	29	76	4/4
I Surrender To You	32	76	4/4
Lead Us Up The Mountain	41	76	4/4
Living Hallelujah	44	76	4/4
When the Tears Fall	64	76	4/4
Whole World In His Hands	66	76	4/4
Worthy, You Are Worthy	68	76	4/4
Yahweh	69	76	4/4
Beauty for Ashes	5	72	4/4
Beauty Of Your Peace	6	72	4/4
The Beauty of Simplicity	7	72	4/4
Every Little Thing	13	72	4/4

Slow

Title	Number	MM	Time Signature
Divine Invitation	15	69	4/4
I Was Blind	33	69	4/4
If I Have Not Love	34	69	4/4
Mighty Is The Power Of The Cross	45	69	4/4
Mountains High	47	69	4/4
Majesty (Here I Am)	43	68	4/4
Unfailing Love	60	68	4/4
Pure Light	55	66	4/4
Who Am I	65	half note = 66	4/4
Spirit Waltz	58	120	3/4

Index of Songs by Project

Notes

WANNA PLAY?

HERE'S HOW...3 new innovative instructional resources from

WORSHIP TOGETHER®

From those who play by ear to the experienced music reader...Now everyone can play many of today's top modern worship songs.

☆ **Songbooks Include:**

Cut Capo Instruction & Charts - Immediately enhance your guitar sound by creating unique voicings with simple chord fingering

Demo CD - Hear the verse, chorus and bridge of each song in a simple guitar/vocal recording

☆ **And Of Course...**

Sheet Music - Standard notation for piano, vocal and guitar

Chord Charts - Lyric with chord names and diagrams

Overhead Masters and Key & Tempo Indexes

Be sure to collect volumes 1 and 2 to complete the set.

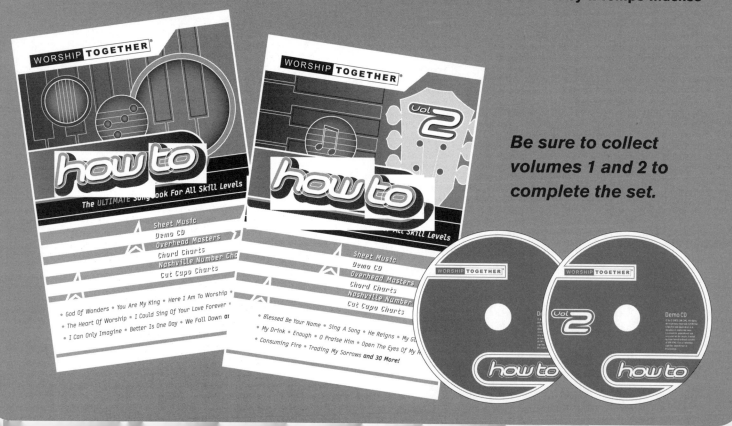

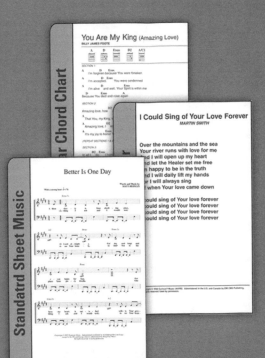

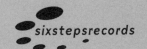

OTHER GREAT RESOURCES FROM WORSHIP TOGETHER.com

HERE I AM TO WORSHIP
VOLUMES 1 AND 2

FEATURES RISING CCLI WORSHIP SONGS EMERGING IN THE UK AND THE US

SONGS FROM: Chris Tomlin, Tim Hughes, Newboys, Matt Redman, Vicky Beeching, Twila Paris, Something Like Silas and more!

HERE I AM TO WORSHIP FOR KIDS
VOLUMES 1 AND 2

RECORDED BY KIDS, FOR KIDS, BRINGING THE TOP WORSHIP SONGS INTO YOUR KIDS LIVES

ALSO AVAILABLE

TIM HUGHES
WHEN SILENCE FALLS

MATT REDMAN
FACEDOWN

CHRIS TOMLIN
ARRIVING

DAVID CROWDER*BAND
ILLUMINATE

PASSION
HYMNS: ANCIENT AND MODERN

BOOKS:

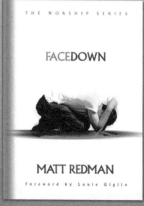

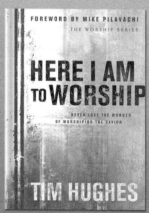

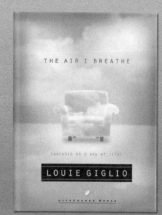

MATT REDMAN
FACEDOWN
FROM REGAL BOOKS

TIM HUGHES
HERE I AM TO WORSHIP
FROM REGAL BOOKS

LOUIE GIGLIO
THE AIR I BREATHE
FROM MULTNOMAH BOOKS